College Plann

An Interactive Workbook Designed to Prepare Students for College

Dymensions Educational Consulting LLC

Cover Design: Justin Carey

Table of Contents

Contributing Authors

Dynette A. Davis, M.Ed, ABD is the CEO of Dymensions Educational Consulting LLC. As an advocate for education, she is committed to interrupting traditional views that stifle growth in the classroom and prevent student, parent, and teacher positive relationships. Dynette has served as a teacher, mentor, curriculum developer, teacher leader, and administrator for both the private and public school sectors. Dynette is currently teaching full-time with Strayer University. Driven by her passion for education, she has developed and implemented unique academic programs, researched educational policy, and designed teacher readiness programs to promote academic improvement. Dynette received her undergraduate degree from DePaul University, in Child Psychology and holds two Master degrees in Elementary Education and Curriculum and Instruction from Concordia University-Chicago. She is currently completing her doctorate degree in Higher Educational Leadership with Concordia University-Chicago. Away from her career responsibilities and academic goals, Dynette enjoys the company of her daughters Sasha and Londyn.

DYMENSIONS
Educational Consulting LLC

Christy Dorsey, M.A. is a motivational speaker and college consultant, born and raised on Chicago's west side. Christy is no stranger to struggle and uses her real life experiences paired with her nurturing ways to inspire young people in the Chicagoland area as well as other major U.S cities. Her strong views on college completion led her to complete her B.A and M.A degrees in Communications and Training from Governors State University. Christy has more than ten years of experience in and around college admissions. Assisting first generation students has been and will always be her personal focus. She currently works alongside her daughter, Aiyana as the President/CEO of The Concrete Rose Society. She also works as a fitness instructor with KaribFit, a Caribbean-inspired fitness class that will soon make its debut in Chicago. Christy's motto is 'Be the Change You Seek' and she lives this motto day in and day out.

Tiffanie Jeffrey, MSW, M.Ed studied Psychology at Northwestern University and received her Master's degree in Social Work from Loyola University Chicago. She started her career in education as a school social worker and has diligently lent her expertise to various school settings in both suburban and urban areas. She realized that she was destined to do so much more in the school system, and went on to pursue her Masters in Educational Leadership and Professional Administrative Licensure from Lewis University. Currently, Tiffanie works for a special education cooperative in northern DuPage County as a Special Education Administrator and Behavioral Consultant. Because of her love for lifelong learning, Tiffanie is continuing her education as she is currently working on obtaining her Doctorate degree in Special Education. Outside of work and school, Tiffanie is a devoted wife and mother of two beautiful boys.

DYMENSIONS
Educational Consulting LLC

Apryl M. Moore, MHRM is the founder of Money Mom Inc., Creator of the Visionary Moms Club, Author, Speaker, Wealth Building Educator, Mom Manager, Visionary Mom, and a thought leader for Moms and children in the areas of financial education, entrepreneurship, parenting, and legacy building. Apryl equips Moms with the tools needed to create their legacy and educate their children to become the leaders that they will someday depend on. Known to many as "Money Mom" and now a "Visionary Mom", Apryl is dedicated to educating and inspiring Moms on teaching their children about financial responsibility, the benefits of parent involvement, and how that builds a lasting legacy. Apryl is also an advocate for youth entrepreneurship and is successfully raising and mentoring her own daughter to become a successful entrepreneur, author (Raising the Boss), and inspirational speaker.

DYMENSIONS
Educational Consulting LLC

Dr. Ro is an international leader in educational leadership. She began her career as a teacher of middle school students with special needs and has taught all levels, including undergraduate and graduate courses at the University of North Texas. Audiences enjoy Dr. Ro's wit as she pushes the boundaries of how to improve educational outcomes of students. Her areas of expertise include special education advocacy, school design, culturally proficient leadership, and teacher development. Dr. Ro holds a Bachelor of Science in Elementary and Special Education from Grambling State University, Master of Education in Special Education, and Doctor of Education in Educational Leadership and Higher Education Administration from the University of North Texas. Dr. Ro is the proud mother of two college students, Michael and Mia—her greatest achievements.

DYMENSIONS
Educational Consulting LLC

Introduction

DYMENSIONS EDUCATIONAL CONSULTING, LLC is committed to the continued development in the field of education for students, parents, and educators. Our mission is to promote change through re-establishing parent-teacher relationships, offering professional development opportunities for educators, and developing academic programs throughout the education community.

The Path to College

Acceptance into a college or university is a major accomplishment. It is the result of hard work and dedication performed by students, with the support of parents and educators. While college acceptance offers a sense of accomplishment for students, it is the years of preparation and sacrifice that make everything possible. There are many components that will require the attention of everyone involved in a student's college preparation process. The purpose of this workbook is to provide a resource that will ensure the correct steps are taken on the path of college preparation.

This workbook will guide you through an interactive process to:

- Create a profile for college application use.

- Complete a yearly checklist for college preparation.

- Identify colleges and universities that offer the best academic options.

- Complete higher education applications.

- Develop a solid plan for college completion.

- Prepare academically for college acceptance.

- Assess career planning, work interests, values, skills, personality type, and leisure time interests.

- Create a financial plan that includes college scholarship opportunities.

DYMENSIONS
Educational Consulting LLC

Before you begin to complete the contents of this workbook, let's put together a profile that will help make your application process and scholarship search seamless. Many applications and scholarships will require the same information. Having it included in one document, will make the process less time consuming. Use the template on the following pages to complete your initial profile for college preparation. Your profile will grow throughout your high school career. You will also participate in different clubs and activities that can be added. Remember to write everything down. When the time comes for you to begin the application process, the completed document will allow you to see how hard you have worked over the years. Most college admissions teams look at different factors when considering an application. Every student brings unique experiences to the application process. Make sure colleges and universities remember your name.

Academic Profile

Personal Information

Name: _____

Date of Birth: _____   Social Security Number: _____

Male: _____   Female: _____ (check one)

Address: _____

City: _____   ST: _____   Zip: _____

Email: _____
(Create a first and last name email that can be used for applications and professional purposes)

Home Phone: _____   Cell Phone: _____

Parent/Guardian Information

Name: _____

Date of Birth: _____   Social Security Number: _____

Mother: _____   Father: _____ (check one)

Address: _____

City: _____   ST: _____   Zip: _____

Email: _____

Home Phone: _____   Cell Phone: _____

Social Media Page Information
(Make sure your social media pages are free from anything that will prevent college acceptance)

Twitter: _____

Instagram: _____

Snapchat: _____

Facebook: _____

LinkedIn: _____

School Information

High School Name: _____

Address: _____

School Counselor: _____

City: _____ ST: _____ Zip: _____

Website: _____

Office Phone: _____ Fax: _____

GPA: 9th _____ 10th _____ 11th _____ 12th _____

Class Rank: _____ / _____

Standardized Test Scores:

ACT ____ Date Taken: ____ SAT ____ Date Taken: ____ State Test ____ Date Taken: ____

Academic Honors and Awards:

_____

_____

_____

_____

Work Experience

Company Name:	_____	*Address:*	_____
Job Title:	_____	*City/ST/ZIP:*	_____
Responsibilities:	_____	*Phone:*	_____
	_____	*Supervisor Name:*	_____
	_____	*Dates of Employment:*	_____

Work Experience

Company Name:	_____	*Address:*	_____
Job Title:	_____	*City/ST/ZIP:*	_____
Responsibilities:	_____	*Phone:*	_____
	_____	*Supervisor Name:*	_____
	_____	*Dates of Employment:*	_____

Clubs and Activities: _____

                                           _____

Academic Achievements: _____   .

_____

_____

Extracurricular Experience: _____

_____

_____

Volunteer Activities: _____

_____

Special Skills: _____

_____

_____

Summer Enrichment: _____

_____

Hobbies and Interests: _____

_____

DYMENSIONS
Educational Consulting LLC

Community Service

Freshmen Year:

Organization Name: _____

Service Dates: _____

Supervisor Name: _____

Supervisor Phone: _____

Supervisor Email: _____

Supervisor Signature: _____ Date: _____

Sophomore Year:

Organization Name: _____

Service Dates: _____

Supervisor Name: _____

Supervisor Phone: _____

Supervisor Email: _____

Supervisor Signature: _____ Date: _____

Junior Year:

Organization Name: _____

Service Dates: _____

Supervisor Name: _____

Supervisor Phone: _____

Supervisor Email: _____

Supervisor Signature: _____ Date: _____

Senior Year:

Organization Name: _____

Service Dates: _____

Supervisor Name: _____

Supervisor Phone: _____

Supervisor Email: _____

Supervisor Signature: _____   Date: _____

Why do you want to go to college?

_____

_____

_____

_____

_____

_____

_____

_____

_____

_____

DYMENSIONS
Educational Consulting LLC

Chapter 1:   ACADEMIC PREPARATION

High School Academics

Graduation Requirements

College readiness depends on more than knowledge and skills in English and Math. Technical courses and other academia are also considered essential by colleges and universities. Students must show their ability to handle a rigorous and well-rounded curriculum. Taking a variety of classes to show your wide knowledge base in academic and technical skills is essential.

Graduation requirements vary from state to state. It is important to understand the courses that you are expected to take and pass during high school. Remember to maintain a good relationship with your high school counselor as he/she will probably be the first to know of any changes with your requirements. As you begin to select the college that you wish to attend, be sure to compare their acceptance criteria with your high school's graduation requirements. Meeting graduation requirements does not guarantee acceptance into a college or university.

ACTIVITY:

Use the chart below to write your high school graduation requirements and the acceptance criteria of a college that interests you.

My High School Graduation Requirements	College Acceptance Criteria
•	•
•	•
•	•
•	•
•	•

Interpreting your GPA

GPA stands for Grade Point Average. All students receive a cumulative GPA at the end of their first semester and second semester each year. Each letter grade received earns an honor point value. All honors points received throughout high school are averaged together in order to compute the cumulative GPA. GPA is calculated using either a 4.0 (unweighted) scale or 5.0 (weighted) scale. Grades earned in driver education and courses taken on a pass/fail basis are not used in computing GPA.

Why do I need to know this? This information will help with:

- Acceptance to college
- Future financial aid, which requires "satisfactory academic progress"
- Scholarship eligibility
- Future employment opportunities
- Eligibility for college athletic teams
- Eligibility for sororities, fraternities and other organizations

Calculating your GPA

Weighted vs. Unweighted Cumulative GPA

Unweighted Cumulative GPA is the average of your final grades received based on a 4.0 scale (see table below).

Grades	Points
A (90%-100%)	4
B (80%-89%)	3
C (70%-79%)	2
D (60%-69%)	1
F (0%-59%)	0

DYMENSIONS
Educational Consulting LLC

Unweighted GPA is calculated by multiplying the final course grade with the credit awarded divided by the total credits.

Example

Course	Final Grade	Credit	Points
Chemistry	B	1.0	3
Algebra 2	C	1.0	2
Pottery	A	1.0	4
Health	A	.5	2
P.E.	A	.5	2
Technology Application	B	1.0	3
English 2	B	1.0	3
Geometry	C	1.0	2
U.S. Government	B	1.0	3
Total		8.0	24
	Unweighted GPA=24/8.0		3.0

Record your schools "unweighted" grade point system below.

Grade	Points
A	
B	
C	
D	
F	

Calculate your UNWEIGHTED GPA.

Course	Final Grade	Credit	Points
Total			
	Unweighted GPA=		

DYMENSIONS
Educational Consulting LLC

Weighted Cumulative GPA uses a different scale based on the "weight" of certain courses. Some courses (i.e. honors courses and International Baccalaureate courses) are calculated on the weighted 5.0 scale to determine your weighted GPA.

Grade	Points
A (90%-100%)	5.00
B (80%-89%)	3.75
C (70%-79%)	3.50
D (60%-69%)	1.25
F (0%-59%)	0

Calculating weighted (5.0 scale) cumulative GPA's: [Quality Points = Grade Points x Credits Earned]

Course	Final Grade	Credit	Weighted	Points
Chemistry	B	1.0	Y	3.75
Algebra 2	C	1.0	Y	2.50
Pottery	A	1.0	N	4.00
Health	A	.5	N	2.00
P.E.	A	.5	N	2.00
Technology Application	B	1.0	N	3.00
English 2	B	1.0	Y	3.75
Geometry	C	1.0	Y	2.50
U.S. Government	B	1.0	Y	3.75
Total		8.0		27.25
	Unweighted GPA=27.25/8.0			3.4063

Calculate your WEIGHTED GPA.

Course	Final Grade	Credit	Weighted	Points
Total				
	Unweighted GPA=			

College Readiness Standards

College Readiness Standards are detailed, research-based descriptions of the knowledge that you are likely to know and are able to understand before you enter college. These standards have been developed for the following content areas: English, Mathematics, Reading, and Science.

Why were the standards developed? These Standards were developed in response to the need for better information about student achievement and to answer the often-asked question, "What does a given score on EXPLORE, PLAN, or the ACT really mean?" The Standards serve as a direct link between what students have learned, what they are ready to learn next, and what they must learn before leaving high school in order to be prepared for college. The Standards are an effective tool for enhancing student learning based on test scores that students earn. The Standards are complemented by ideas for progress— brief descriptions of learning experiences from which students might benefit. Remember, to be successful in college takes tenacity, support from friends and family, and your determination.

College Entrance Exams

As you prepare for college, you will encounter at least one (and probably more than one) of the following college entrance exams:

- PSAT/NMSQT: Preliminary Scholastic Aptitude Test/National Merit Scholarship Qualifying Assessment Test
- SAT Reasoning Test
- ACT
- SAT Subject Tests (formerly the SAT II)

Admissions requirements vary from school to school. Consult your prospective school when deciding which test to take. Learn more about each of the tests below:

Test: PSAT/NMSQT

Description: The test is split up into three different sections. You will have 60 minutes to answer 47 reading questions, 35 minutes to answer 44 writing questions/tasks, and 70 minutes on 48 math questions. Like the new SAT, you will not be penalized for wrong answers — or for guessing. This test is not used to determine college admissions. It is instead intended to help students prepare for the SAT. It has the same format as the SAT, but shorter – a test of verbal and mathematical reasoning.

Usually Taken: During your sophomore year, though you may wish to take it sooner for practice.

Tips and Strategies: If you do well on the PSAT (and meet additional academic requirements), you may qualify for the National Merit Scholarship Program (a nationally distributed merit-based scholarship). Only scores from the junior year are used to determine qualification for National Merit Program. For more information visit the College Board website. (See website reference page)

Test: SAT Reasoning Test

Description: Scale ranging from 200 to 800 for Evidence-Based Reading and Writing; 200 to 800 for Math; 2 to 8 on each of three dimensions for written essay. Essay results are reported separately. The test is split into three different sections. You will have 65 minutes to answer 52 reading questions, 35 minutes to answer 44 writing questions/tasks, 80 minutes on 58 math questions, and 50 minutes for the essay.

Usually Taken: Spring of your junior year or fall of your senior year (or both, if you want a practice run).

Tips and Strategies: It used to be that the SAT carries a "wrong answer penalty". If you guessed right, you gained a point; if you guessed wrong, you were penalized. Now, you can guess without risking your SAT score. You can retake the test to improve your score, but all available scores are sent to your prospective colleges, including the results of tests you have taken previously. The SAT does not allow students to send only their latest and/or best scores.

Test: ACT

Description: Three-hour exam; 215 questions; measures achievement in English, Math, Reading and Science. The ACT Plus includes an optional 40-minute writing test. Scores on each section are averaged to create a composite score. A perfect score is 36. Students in the Midwest and South generally take the ACT.

Usually Taken*:* Spring of your junior year or fall of your senior year (or both, if you want a practice run).

Tips and Strategies: Your score is based on the number of correct answers ONLY. If you aren't sure, take a guess – it can't hurt you and it could help. Harder questions are worth the same amount as easy ones. Answer the easy questions first and leave the more time-consuming questions until the end. For more information visit the ACT website. (See website reference page)

Test: SAT Subject Tests

Description: One-hour test that assesses mastery of a particular field of study. Up to three tests can be required for admissions. Some schools use the SAT II for course placement; others don't require it at all. Tests are offered in five subject areas: English, Math, History, Science and Foreign Language. Scores are based on an 800-point scale.

Usually Taken: After you have finished the relevant course work (can be as early as freshman or sophomore year, depending on the school's curriculum and the student's progress).

Tips and Strategies: Entrance requirements vary from college to college. Consult with your guidance counselor or college admissions representative to determine which tests you should take.

DYMENSIONS
Educational Consulting LLC

Choosing the Right Courses

Selecting classes in high school is different than college. In high school, your curriculum is generic and does not offer a wide range of courses to select. In college, you have the opportunity to select from hundreds of classes in a specialized area.

Meet with your Counselor: High School Counselors help students decide which classes to take. It is important to meet with your counselor before you register for classes each year. Come with a list of questions.

Use College Credits and Placement Exams: If you are planning to earn college credits in high school—for example, through the AP or IB programs—find out if you can use them to fulfill any core requirements before you register. You can also test out of required courses by scoring well on a college placement exam.

If a number of tests are scheduled then you have a shorter amount of time to study for each exam and your schedule should reflect this. This also means the tests will demand more memory skill and recollection of details.

- You may have to create study block.

- Create study tools for recall. It is essential that daily review of notes and tools take place for better recall and association of material. With a short time between exams you must find ways to associate the material and consistently connect it to the previous day's lecture. You need to do more than recognize what is being asked, you must be able to identify it and give specific details (often times dates, names, places, examples).

The Day of the Exam

- Get to the testing center a few minutes early so that you can settle in and not feel rushed.

- Before you start the exam, look at the entire test. How many multiple choice, short answer, and essay questions are there on the exam? For example, say it is a 60 minute test and there are 20 multiple choice, 10 short answer (fill in), and one essay (needing two examples) questions. How much time will you need for each section? You need to schedule at least 5 minutes to write an outline for the essay, 30 seconds per multiple choice questions, and one minute per fill in question. That gives you 25 minutes for the essay which usually carries the most points.

- Start the exam, go through and answer all that is familiar. If you get to a multiple choice question and you are unsure of the answer, put a check mark next to it and move on. The key is to answer as many as you can in a set amount of time for maximum points. The more you answer the more confident you will become. Go from question to question - do not go backwards - you will answer those you are unsure of at the end of the exam if there is time left.

It is wise to answer the multiple choice questions first because these questions hold varied information that may answer the fill in questions and/or give examples for the essay.

The Multiple Choice Exams

Many students fail multiple-choice exams because the expectation is that the questions will be straight forward and easily recognized. Most teachers develop multiple-choice questions by synthesizing material from more than one source creating a dual layered question demanding analysis of the question rather than rote memory.

- Read the question.

- If the question is long, underline the subject and verb to help you focus appropriately.

- Read each possible answer without bias. Do not stop and think about the answer - just read each answer.

- Now, focus on the answer you think is correct. If there is more than one (should only be two at the most) reread the question and make sure you understand the words and what they mean in the question. Look at the answers again and decide. If you can't, put a check next to it and move on. Do not stop and waste three minutes on one multiple-choice question that by itself is only worth maybe two points.

- Evaluate whether the answer choices are giving general or specific information. If you can think of an exception for the specific statement then the general statement is usually correct.

- Read the question carefully and underline negative (not, never, neither) or affirmative words (always, all, only). This usually signifies that the answer must be specific fact rather than a general statement.

- If you have time at the end of the exam, go back and answer those questions that you placed check marks next to. Do not change the answers to those already completed!

- Periodically check to make sure the scantron question number matches the test number. It is very easy to get distracted and start marking the wrong test question. Stay alert!

True-False Questions

Look for open and closed words in the question. Open words like often or usually are found in true statements whereas closed words like never and always are often found in false statements.

Pay attention to statements with two clauses - both must be true in order to be the correct answer.

Subjective Tests

These are exams that are opinion based but answers may vary from student to student dependent upon examples used or details given.

Subjective tests are usually more general in nature than objective tests but specific facts and organization are expected. Recall rather than memorization is the skill used to answer these types of exams. It is better to understand the general concepts of the issue with a few well-learned details than a large repertoire of unorganized material that seems unrelated when presented.

When preparing for essay exams you should write down the main topics discussed in the assigned chapters of the texts and presented in your notes. Make sure you understand the general concepts of each topic (know who, what, when, where, why) and provide at least two examples. Recite the material out loud in your own words to ensure recall and comprehension. Reread and review the areas in the text where there is limited understanding and comprehension.

Short Answer

- These are similar to essay questions in that you should take a few seconds to write out the example or terms you want to use in the answer. If it is a fill in question, you should move through them fast, answering those that you easily recall. Often times the answers can be found in the multiple choice area but you do not want to spend too much time trying to figure out the answer. Keep in mind how much each question is worth in points and how many points you will lose if you take too much time on one question.

Essay Exams

- Carefully read the question. Break the question into parts so you know what you need to answer for full credit.

- Note what type of question is being asked - compare and contrast, analyze and comment.

- Take the time to create an outline on your answer sheet so that even if you don't complete the essay the teacher can see where you were going and may give you points. Although you are taking a few minutes away from answering the essay, it will increase your chances for a more coherent answer with examples that flow and an essay that makes sense. Use the parts of the essay to help create the outline - this will help with organization and keep you focused on topic.

- Follow your outline and begin the essay. Write straight through and do not vary from the outline. You took the time to write it out so trust it. If you try to change the direction of your essay, you end up with a difficult to read essay. The easier your essay is to read and the better it flows, the easier it will be for your teacher to follow your train of thought.

- Reread the directions and make sure you answered the entire question(s). And if you still have time, reread your essay and correct spelling and grammatical errors.

The Exam Isn't Over When You Turn It In

Taking the exam is only the first part to assessing what you know. The second part comes with the return of the exam. At this time you have the prime opportunity to see what you knew and learn what you didn't. You should always go back and find out why you missed particular questions, what type of questions they were, did you answer the whole questions or only part, then find the correct answer, and write it out so you know it. This is especially useful if you will be taking a comprehensive final. Make sure you talk with the teacher about how you can improve in a particular area or ask why they worded the question the way they did.

Test Anxiety

What is it?

Most students experience some level of anxiety. When it interferes with test performance, it is deemed excessive and labeled test anxiety. Test anxiety is often defined in physiological terms: sweaty palms, going blank, and butterflies in the stomach. (Cizek & Burg, 2006)

If test anxiety goes beyond the physiological, and it consistently interferes with performance then you may want to seek additional assistance from the school psychologist or counselor to gain a better understanding.

DYMENSIONS
Educational Consulting LLC

What are ways to reduce?

- Assess your study skills and develop areas that are weaker to ensure successful learning efficiency.

- Be prepared. The more time you give yourself to prepare and learn the material the more confident you will feel the day of the exam.

- Stay organized and on task. Keep to a schedule so that you give yourself enough time to study.

- Get enough sleep starting before the exam.

- Stay hydrated.

- Exercise to eliminate stress.

- Eat well balanced meals. Make sure you eat breakfast or lunch before the exam with at least 20 minutes to digest.

- Stay relaxed.

Test Anxiety and the day of the exam:

- Give yourself enough time to get to the exam and find a comfortable seat (If not assigned). Get your writing utensils out, take a couple of minutes to close your eyes and take a couple of deep breaths.

- Do not discuss test material with other students.

- Do not bring your class materials with you.

Test Anxiety and taking the exam:

- Remember your test taking strategies - review the exam.

- Occasionally stretch so that your body stays relaxed.

- If you go blank, put your pencil down, sit up straight, take two or three deep breaths, then pick up your pencil again, and begin. If you don't immediately recognize the question, go to the next.

- Stay positive and remind yourself that you studied appropriately and that you know the material.

- Remind yourself that some anxiety is normal and that you know the material.

- Don't pay attention to others students or if they turn in their exams before you. You do not get points for being the first one to turn in your exam.

Interpreting Exam Scores

It doesn't matter if you don't get a perfect score! While a less-than-perfect score doesn't mean you won't get into the top colleges, a perfect score doesn't mean you will. Some schools have actually wait-listed or deferred a few applicants who have gotten perfect test scores, and it's likely that other schools have as well.

The percentiles for the SAT vary from year to year. They are not like grades in school; a 90th percentile score doesn't mean you get an "A." Rather, the percentiles have to do with a comparison of groups of students from year to year. If you score in the 68th percentile on the math section means you did better than approximately 68 percent of your state's college-bound seniors the year prior. You'll get a percentile score for the total group of test-takers and for your state. (Herrnstein & Murray, 2010)

Test-Taking Strategies for Success

On the first day of class your teacher will pass out a syllabus that explains what the course will focus on. Look at the syllabus and notice:

- How many tests are scheduled for the term and how far apart are they - one midterm/one final, three midterms/one final. This information helps you assess how much information will need to be learned for each exam.

- Ask your teacher questions about exams on the first day of class so that you can adjust how you study for the class:

o   What kinds of exams are given - Objective, Essay, Multiple Choice, True/False, or Varied?

o   If varied, how many of each type of question?

o   How much time is given to take the exam - the entire class period, half the class period...?

With this information, you can set a realistic schedule for each class by breaking down the readings and tasks in appropriate blocks for maximum learning efficiency. For example, if it is a class that only has two exams, one midterm and one final, you have a number of weeks to learn the material and your schedule for this class should:

- Break down reading assignments in two or three parts each week,

- Allow time for daily review of notes and highlighted areas of text for better recall,

- Allow for time to create term and definition cards as a memory aid,

- Allow time for study group discussions,

- Create test questions to help you actively think about the exam: use your notes, comments made in the margins while reading, turn the text subheadings into questions. Practice essay exams can cover large sections of information compared to practicing with objective tests that are detail specific.

DYMENSIONS
Educational Consulting LLC

Students with Special Needs

The Americans with Disabilities Act (ADA) ensures that students with disabilities have equal access to post-secondary education programs, services and facilities. Whether you decide to go to a four-year university or a two-year career school, you shouldn't rule out any future education options because of a physical or mental disability. (Kochhar-Bryant & Izzo, 2006)

As a student with disabilities, it is important to thoroughly understand federal, state, and local rights. Exploring the resources available to you on campus can make the transition to college much easier. If you qualify for academic adjustments, speak to an admissions advisor early so you can receive services and/or assistive technology when classes begin. Many colleges employ ADA or disability rights coordinators and disability services staff who can serve as on-campus resources for your needs. There are services that are available for students who are eligible to receive special accommodations.

Know Your Rights

Section 504 of the Rehabilitation Act of 1973 (De Fabrique, 2011) is one of the earliest federal pieces of disability rights legislation and its roots can be traced backed to civil rights demonstrations by the American Coalition of Citizens with Disabilities (ACCD). Through public sit-ins, lobbying, and activist demonstrations, ACCD was able to sway Jimmy Carter's administration to ensure Section 504 compliance, which, in turn, paved the way for subsequent amendments. (Evans, 2017) Students attending college must be provided with equal access to classrooms, and they may be deemed eligible for accommodations.

DYMENSIONS
Educational Consulting LLC

At first glance, it can be difficult to tell if you are covered by the protections granted in Section 504. According to the legal text, the law applies to a "qualified individual with a disability." So how does the OCR determine whether you apply? The provisions define qualified individuals as those with a physical or mental condition that substantially restricts one or more major life activities. (McCrea, 2014) The Department of Education (DOE) provides some examples of these types of impairments. However, please keep in mind that this is not a comprehensive list:

- Neurological conditions
- Sense organ impairments
- Musculoskeletal impairments
- Emotional or mental illnesses
- Respiratory conditions
- Digestive ailments
- Learning disabilities
- Organic brain syndromes

If you receive Special Education Services or 504 accommodations, you may consider the following steps for planning to attend college:

DYMENSIONS
Educational Consulting LLC

Make a list of the services you'll need for a successful education

Before you look for the colleges that can accommodate you best, you need to know what you are looking for and understand your rights for education according to the ADA. When planning for college, consider what programs and services you will need from special transportation to and from classes, including extra time for exams.

Find colleges to match your needs

While schools must accommodate your needs, you may find more success at a college or university that already has special programs and services in place. Find colleges based on your desired degree, and then request information on their current programs for students with disabilities. You should evaluate schools based on your special needs. You can find disability programs at a variety of colleges and universities.

Be prepared to show documentation regarding the diagnosis of your disability.

Check with your future school to see what is required. If you do not have the documentation your school requires, you may need to get a new evaluation.

Tips & Tactics for Students with Disabilities

- Do not wait for schools to contact you about special accommodations. Be proactive and initiate any requests.

- Once you choose a school and begin your program, make appointments with your instructors to ensure you get the accommodations you need.

- Develop a support system of other students with disabilities. A study group of students with similar needs can help you stay on track and increase your learning.

Complete the chart to help you plan.

Make a list of the services you'll need for a successful education:	List campus specialists contact information:
Find and list colleges to match your needs:	Research and list scholarships for students with disabilities:

Research and list documentation needed regarding the diagnosis of your disability.	Gather additional resources

Notes:

_____

_____

_____

_____

_____

_____

_____

_____

_____

DYMENSIONS
Educational Consulting LLC

Student Services

Colleges and universities support students with disabilities and special needs in a variety of ways. Contact the Office of Services for Students with Disabilities at the college of your choice. This office is designed to support the University's commitment to equality and diversity by providing support services and academic accommodations to students with disabilities. Information is shared to promote awareness of disability issues and provide support within the community.

Study Habits

The key to becoming an effective student is learning how to study smarter, not harder. You will learn this as you advance in your education. An hour or two of studying a day is usually sufficient to make it through high school with satisfactory grades, but when college arrives, there aren't enough hours in the day to get all your studying in if you do not know how to study smarter.

Describe your study habits.

_____

_____

_____

_____

_____

DYMENSIONS
Educational Consulting LLC

Now take a look at my top 5 habits of highly effective college students. (Rodriguez, 2016)

Make sure you are not distracted while studying	Plan when you are going to study.	Study at the same time.

Each study time should have a specific goal.	Never procrastinate your planned study session.

What changes do you need to make in your study habits?

_____

_____

_____

_____

_____

_____

_____

Chapter 2:   COLLEGE PLANNING

College admissions teams look at a wide range of factors when considering your application. Every student brings unique experiences to the application process. Your college planning process will have a few requirements that will need your attention. Planning early will eliminate stress that comes with having to make last minute decisions.

Coursework

The courses listed below should prepare you for success in college and beyond.

Take **English** every year. Traditional courses, such as American and English literature, help improve your writing skills, reading comprehension and vocabulary.

Algebra and **Geometry** help you succeed on college entrance exams and in college math classes. Take them early, so you'll have time for advanced science and math, which will help show colleges you are ready for higher-level work.

Most colleges want students with three years of high school math. The more competitive colleges prefer four years. Take some combination of the following:

- Algebra I
- Algebra II
- Geometry
- Trigonometry
- Calculus

DYMENSIONS
Educational Consulting LLC

Take at least five solid academic classes every semester.

Science teaches you how to think analytically and how to apply theories to reality. Colleges want to see that you have taken at least three years of laboratory science classes. A good combination includes a year of each of the following:

- Biology
- Chemistry or Physics
- Earth/space science

Schools that are more competitive expect four years of lab science courses, which you may be able to get by taking advanced classes in these same areas. Improve your understanding of local and world events by studying the cultures and history that helped shape them. Here is a suggested high school course plan:

- U.S. History (a full year)
- U.S. Government (half a year)
- World History Geography (half a year)
- An extra half-year in the above or other areas

Solid foreign language study shows that you're willing to stretch beyond the basics. Many colleges require at least two years of study in the same foreign language, and some prefer more. Research indicates that students who participate in the arts often do better in school and on standardized tests. The arts help you recognize patterns, learn to notice differences and similarities, and exercise your mind in unique ways. Many colleges require or recommend one or two semesters in the arts. Good choices include studio art, dance, music and drama.

Social Media

What you post online can play a major role in your admission process. Social media has become another tool that college admissions teams use for their selection process. Social media is the new resume. You may not know how poor judgement could affect your college and career choices. Posting opinions about religious and political views could be damaging to your image and offend someone. Make sure everything that you post represents you well. Below is an online self-assessment. Take a few minutes to complete tasks regarding your online presence.

- Google yourself to see what information comes up. Include key words that can help your search.

- Delete any inappropriate photos or language that you may have posted in the past.

- If you have friends that have posted any negative material of you, ask them to remove it from their social media accounts.

- Make sure you are not tagged in anything inappropriate.

ACTIVITY:

Respond to the prompts below.

When college representatives search for me, I would like for them to find the following information:

_____

_____

I need to clean up the following things:

_____

_____

_____

DYMENSIONS
Educational Consulting LLC

You can begin completing a yearly checklist during your freshman year of high school. Regardless of where you enter this process, it is important to follow each step below.

Freshman Checklist

1. *Determine what GPA is needed for the college selection that you have made.*

2. *Research and write down the state's graduation requirements.*

3. *Start looking for scholarships.*

4. *Research and list a minimum of three careers that you would consider for your future.*

5. *Sit down with your high school counselor to discuss future career goals and possible colleges that would help you achieve each goal.*

6. *Create a community service schedule to obtain hours throughout high school.*

Sophomore Checklist

1. *Register to take the PSAT and PACT.*

2. *Attend college fairs to get information about schools and what they offer.*

3. *Determine what GPA is needed for the college selection that you have made.*

4. *Research and write down the state's graduation requirements.*

5. *Research and write for scholarships.*

6. *Research and list a minimum of three careers that you would consider for your future.*

7. *Sit down with your high school counselor to discuss future career goals and possible colleges that would help you achieve each goal.*

8. *Create a community service schedule to obtain hours throughout high school.*

9. *Create a list of ten schools have the major you are interested in pursuing.(see College Interest chart)*

Junior Checklist

1. *Register to take the ACT and SAT.*

2. *Attend college fairs to get information about schools and what they offer.*

3. *Determine what GPA is needed for the college selection that you have made.*

4. *Research and write down the state's graduation requirements.*

5. *Research and write for scholarships.*

6. *Work on college essays.*

7. *Apply for scholarships.*

Senior Checklist

1. *Work on college essays.*

2. *Apply to selected colleges by application deadline.*

3. *Register to take the ACT and SAT.*

4. *File the FAFSA(Free Application for Federal Student Aid)*

5. *Apply for scholarships*

DYMENSIONS
Educational Consulting LLC

Chapter 3:   CHOOSING THE RIGHT COLLEGE

Choosing the right college should be a fun process. If the selection process is done correctly, you will have multiple options. When following the traditional path of choosing the right college, high school students must follow the necessary steps to ensure a smooth process. These steps include:

Entrance Requirements

During your high school orientation, you were given a list of requirements. Meeting the requirements will lead to high school completion/graduation. In addition to the high school graduation requirements, each college and university has a set of requirements for admission. It is your responsibility to meet the requirements of both institutions. Knowing the college and university admission requirements prior to starting high school will allow you an opportunity to better plan out your high school courses. For students that are in grades 9th – 11th, an outline of entrance requirements needed should be put into place. Every course you take in high school should prepare you for success in college and beyond.

List of Desired Schools

The next thing on our 'To Do List' is to create a list with names of your desired colleges or universities. High school students select colleges for a variety of reasons. Students should start developing a 'Desired Schools' list as early as possible. As you get closer to your senior year, you should start to narrow down these choices. The list should be based on a number of different variables, for example, consider colleges that have your intended major or colleges that fall within a comfortable price range for you and your family. With proper research, you can compose a solid list of options that meet your specific needs and qualities that you want out of a school.

A good place to start would be by asking some very important questions like what do I want to be when I grow up? What schools are known for the career choice that I have chosen? Do I think the academic culture as well as the on-campus culture will be a rewarding one for me? If the school is out of state, you should start to consider how you will prepare to transition to another state. If the school is in-state, you should consider transportation options that would help you to travel between school and home, when necessary. Other things to consider would be the types of available academic resources and research opportunities. If you are considering financial aid, you may want to research the number of students currently enrolled that receive financial assistance, as well as the types of scholarships that are available for students. These are just a few questions and ideas to get you started with creating your list of top schools. If you are making decisions about colleges to attend without including some of these ideas in your thought process, you may want to reevaluate your list.

Once you have completed a solid list, you can start to prioritize your list. The best way to do that is to figure out which schools best fit your needs. I would definitely suggest creating your list with a pencil so that you can always go back and erase without making the list look messy or disorganized.

Higher Education Requirement Grid Example:

University Requirements	Freshmen	Sophomore	Junior	Senior
4 years of Math	English I	English II	English III	English IV
3 years of Math	Algebra I	Algebra II	Geometry	4th Year Math
3 years of History	World Geography	World History	US History	Government & Economics
3 years of Science	Biology	Chemistry	Physics	4th Year Science
2 years of Foreign Language				

Directions: Use the grid below to identify the classes needed to fulfill the entrance requirements for admission to the colleges or universities of your choice.

Higher Education Requirement Grid

Name of College or University	Requirements	Freshmen	Sophomore	Junior	Senior
	Reading Language Arts				
	Math				
	Science				
	Social Studies				
	Foreign Language				

Note: Take at least five academic classes every semester.

DYMENSIONS
Educational Consulting LLC

Visiting Schools

School visits generally take place after a major of study is selected. During the school visit(s), identify the admission requirements of each institution and compare the results to your current high school academic status. Not every college/university offers the same programs. If you are interested in pursuing a law degree, you should research the pre-law programs that are offered. Every college/university works to offer something unique that will make them stand out among other institutions. Determine what you need when it comes to deciding on the college or university of your choice. Remember, this will be your new home for a minimum of four years.

Use the chart below when visiting your top eight schools. Document important information that will play a part in your decision to apply.

College/University	Enrollment Size	Cost of Attendance	Graduation Rate

DYMENSIONS
Educational Consulting LLC

College Selection

Choosing the right college is an important part of the planning process. Each step in choosing the right college can lead to a successful college career. Each college and university has multiple schools within the system. These schools separate students according to their major. When a major is selected, an application for admission can be completed. Without an area of study selection, only general admission can be granted. General admission is an option that is chosen when a student is unsure of their post college career plans. Making this decision early will eliminate the excess use of financial aid without having a solid plan. Sometimes, college choices are made because of popularity. Students decide to attend a school because a friend or family member may have attended or is currently attending. This is the fastest way to end a college career, before it starts. Everyone has a different path. Your goals should never be a copy of your peers. It is important to select a college based on your career choice. You will learn more about Career Planning in Chapter 6.

Large vs. Small

Academic goals and personality play a large part in the size of your potential college or university selection. It is very important to ensure that the institution you select is a good fit for you. Small colleges and universities have fewer than 1,000 students. Sometimes students prefer to be in a smaller environment. These environments have lower student to teacher ratios. They also include opportunities for students that come from smaller areas to adjust. Attending a small college or university can also prove beneficial to students that come from larger areas. Your choice should be based on your individual needs and should accompany a visit to ensure this is the proper environment for you.

Large colleges and universities have more than 35,000 students. Large colleges include Big Ten institutions. These universities have everything from top athletic programs to multiple degree programs. Along with these major components, come larger classrooms with fewer teacher student interactions. Larger schools offer more programs and activities. They also offer more resources than a smaller institution.

Finding the Perfect Fit

What do you consider to be the perfect fit for you? How do you know if you are a good fit for a "Small" or "Large" college or university? Answer the following questions, to help determine which option would be best for you.

What is the size of your high school? _____.

When you are sitting in the classroom, do you require the attention of your teacher; 3 or more times a week? Explain.

_____

_____

About how many students are in your current classes? _____. Do you interact with these students? Explain.

_____

_____

Do you feel comfortable with emailing or meeting with your teacher? Explain.

_____

_____

College Search

Choosing the right college should be a fun process. If the selection process is done correctly, you will have multiple options. When choosing the right college, the more options you have, the better.

What do you think happens when you can choose more than one college?

_____

_____

In the chart below, list each college in which you would like to express interest. Record your choice of schools and the requirements that you have met during high school. Organize the list according to your attendance preference.

Chart:

School Name	GPA requirement	ACT/SAT requirement

Chapter 4:   APPLYING FOR COLLEGE

Introduction

Once you arrive to your senior year of high school, you become part of the most respected and the most experienced grade in your school. If you utilize this workbook effectively, your work from this point on should not be too difficult.   However, there is still work to be done so let's get started!

Why Should I Apply for College? (What's in it for me?)

There are several responses to this question. One response may be that you should apply for college because it is the next step in your academic progression. One might assume that applying for college is the next obvious step. Others may say that one should apply for college because their family or friends have informed them that pursuing a higher education degree is the expectation. Whatever the reason for your decision, make sure you will be happy with your choice.

ACTIVITY:

List 3 reasons why you desire to attend college?

1. _____

2. _____

3. _____

DYMENSIONS
Educational Consulting LLC

Invaluable Asset

College education is an invaluable asset. Once obtained, the sky is the limit. There is no price tag that can be placed on receiving a quality education. Society has placed a heavy emphasis on education over the years. Most children are already in a school setting by the age of three, if not before. The message to every child is clear, school is important. If you ask children the difference between what they do and what their parents do, most would tell you that their parents go to work while they go to school. Why do we work so hard? There are many answers to this question; in short it is because we want the nice things that the income from good employment can provide.

Increased Employment Opportunity

College is also a good choice because it allows graduates to increase their employment opportunities. There was a time when a good paying job could be obtained with a high school diploma. Over the past few years, a high school diploma is not enough to gain entry level employment. Many corporations are offering incentives and programs like tuition reimbursement to their employees when they enroll in college degree programs. As a nation, we are getting smarter. According to The Week (2011), the IQ of Americans is on a steady rise. During your job search phase, you will find that employers want to hire employees who have achieved a certain level of education. In most cases, a person with a college degree will be considered for a job before someone who does not. The less educated individual could possibly do a better job, but the employer is assuming that the more educated individual is able to offer a level of expertise that the other individual may or may not be able to offer. Obtaining your college education will increase your hiring potential for a larger number of jobs.

Increased Earning Potential

As you begin to start planning for the future that you want, it is equally important to think about where you want to live, what kind of house you would like, what kind of car you want to drive, etc. Even more important than that is to research the costs associated with each. By doing this, you will gain an understanding of exactly how much income you need to earn annually in order to afford the lifestyle that you intend to have in the future. Now let's take a look at some current statistics. The Bureau of Labor

Statistics (2015) reported that the median weekly income for a high school graduate is $678.00. If you multiply that by 4 weeks of work at full pay, an individual can make up to $2,712.00 per month. Earning $2,712.00 every month would potentially equate to an annual income of around $32,544.00. Now, let's consider the earning potential of that same individual if they obtained a Bachelor's degree. On average, that individual could potentially earn $4,137.00 per week, which amounts to $16,548.00 per month. The annual salary for this individual would be $198,576.00. As you study these numbers again, remember that these are just estimates, but they can give you a great start into putting your earning potential in proper perspective.

ACTIVITY: Answer the following questions:
How much do you plan to make per year? _____

How much is your dream house? _____

How much is your dream car? _____

Who Should Apply For College?

Who should apply for college? The simple answer to this question is YOU! Anyone who has completed state requirements for high school graduation should apply for college, enlist in the military, or take up a trade (i.e. electricians, truck drivers, plumbers, hairstylists). Understandably, college is not for everyone, so with that said find your path and get started.

High School Seniors (Public, Private)

According to the Bureau of Labor Statistics (2015), 69.2% of people who graduated from high school went on to attend college. Most students are able to apply for college during their senior year of high school. Senior year is full of deadlines, football games, basketball games, homecoming dances, prom, and of course GRADUATION. With that, there is not much time to attend college visits or research for your top college of choice. Starting the process early will minimize stress. Public and private high schools alike offer students an opportunity to visit their colleges during the school year as an added resource.

Students should take full advantage of college visits, be it lunchroom, classroom, or guidance counselor visits. The more students get to interact with Admissions Counselors from colleges of their choice, the better. Taking this step is vital to the decision-making process because Admissions Counselors can answer questions that the students may have regarding their prospective schools. College fairs are also highly recommended. Most schools have at least one scheduled college fair per year. High schools that do not have scheduled college fairs can send students to their local community colleges. Similar to college visits, college fairs allow prospective students to have several colleges/universities under one roof at the same time. This can also be helpful for students and parents because questions about the application process and admission criteria can be asked at that time.

ACTIVITY:

List 5 colleges or universities that you plan to visit this year:

1. _____

2. _____

3. _____

4. _____

5. _____

Generate 5 questions that you can ask the college representatives at each school.

1. _____

2. _____

3. _____

4. _____

5. _____

Home School Students

High school seniors are not the only students that are applying for college. Homeschool students are also applying for college. Homeschooled students are more likely to attend college than students who attend high schools (Venable, 2011). These students have either completed 100% of the state requirements at home, online, or both. Homeschooled students are as much invested and interested in college education as their peers who attend high school daily according to traditional norms. Most of these students have access to local college fairs, which allows them the opportunity to engage with admissions professionals.

GED Student

Last, but certainly not least, are students who are considered General Education Development (GED) students. These students, for one reason or another, did not complete traditional high school requirements, but have worked hard in an effort to obtain their GED or graduation equivalency diploma. These students may have had previous opportunities to engage with college admissions professionals but some may have not. The best word of advice for GED students who are looking to engage with Admissions Counselors is to attend local college fair or to contact the college directly to find out if they can schedule an on campus visit.

Preparing To Apply For College

Now that we have discussed why one should attend college and who should apply for college, it is now time to get to work. Applying to college takes a lot of thought, preparation, hard work, and can be very time consuming. If you think waiting until the middle or the end of your senior year is a good idea to prepare to apply for college, you are wrong. In fact, the old adage "the early bird gets the worm" should be at the forefront of your mind. Preparation should start on the first day of high school, if not before. Most students are so enamored with the fact that they are in high school during their freshman year, they forget why they are there. In some cases, students are still experiencing a transition period during their first two years of high school. It is important to make every effort to adjust as quickly as possible early on in their high school career so that they can avoid the stresses and worries that come along with low cumulative GPA's.

ACTIVITY:

Reorganize your 'college needs' list to make it fit what you are looking for in your future institution. (i.e.: Are you looking for a research-based institution? Will you benefit from an institution that is "hands on"?)

What is most important to you as it relates to your future college/university?

_____

_____

_____

_____

_____

Application Requirements

Application requirements outline the minimum admissions criteria that colleges/universities deem acceptable. When preparing to apply to a college or university, it is important to know what the expectations are for potential students. Some colleges and universities will have similar application requirements, but each school will identify their specific requirements in their application. While going through the research process to identify your top schools, you should explore the admissions requirements. Missing the smallest item could jeopardize your chances of gaining admission into the college/university of your dreams. Create a list of top schools, and write down application requirements and deadlines. Keep this comprehensive list as you navigate through the application process.

ACTIVITY:

List the application requirements of your top two picks.

Pick #1	Pick #2
Requirements:	Requirements:
•	•
•	•
•	•

DYMENSIONS
Educational Consulting LLC

What are the application deadlines of your top two picks?

Pick #1	Pick #2
Application Deadline:	Application Deadline:

Complete Application

It is finally application time!! This is the first of several steps that will follow. When looking at an application you may feel excited and nervous. This is expected, as you are making a major life decision. It is important to have your parents or another trusted adult present when completing your college applications. This person will provide the additional guidance and support that you will need. Most applications will require very personal information. This information is generally required because your application is an official government application. The best way to identify yourself is to include your social security number. If you have not committed your social security number to memory, you should use this opportunity to start learning it. This will be the first of many occurrences where you will need to know it.

Once you have completed the initial information, you will also need to include demographic information including your address, city, state, and phone number. Most college applications require the number of years of English, Math, Foreign Language, History, Science, Art, and other classes that you have taken.

Colleges may also want to know about any academic awards you have received during your high school years. Take your time and review the academic profile that was provided for you in the beginning of this workbook. Your academic profile should include extracurricular activities, leadership roles and academic awards you have received. Internship and study abroad opportunities are also very important. Your academic profile should give an overall scope of your time in and out of the classroom. Colleges and universities want to see how well-rounded and involved you are in high school. Each application is designed to give them as much insight on who you are and how successful you will be at their institution.

ACTIVITY:

List the names of the clubs and organizations that you have participated in during each year of high school. You can use items listed on your high school profile.

Freshman:

1. _____
2. _____
3. _____

Sophomore:

1. _____
2. _____
3. _____

Junior:

1. _____
2. _____
3. _____

Senior:

1. _____

2. _____

3. _____

How many years of the following have you completed?

Number of English years: _____

Number of Math years: _____

Number of Science years: _____

Number of Social Studies years: _____

Online Applications

There are two ways that students can apply to colleges and universities. The first and possibly the most popular way at this time is to apply online. College seeking students should be able to obtain access to each college's website. The student would then need to ensure that they complete the application in its entirety before submitting. While completing the application, please be aware of any misspelled words or numbers that could potentially threaten the validity of your application. Should an error occur after you have submitted the application, you should contact the Admissions Office of the respective college to see how the error can be rectified. Once you have completed the application, it is always best to review all of your responses to the requested application questions. Once again, refer back to your list to ensure that you have applied to all of your top pick colleges and universities. A great option for college-seeking students is the Common Application. This website allows students to send applications out to over 700 colleges and universities, in most cases, with a click of the mouse. Although some institutions require essays and additional information with the completed application, it is, for the most part, a very simple way to gain access to hundreds of colleges at the same time. Not every college/university is available on the Common Application.

ACTIVITY:

Write the confirmation numbers of your top schools after your application has been submitted.

School Name	Application Confirmation Number

DYMENSIONS
Educational Consulting LLC

Paper Applications

The second way to apply for college includes the traditional paper application. Typically, the only way to obtain paper applications is to visit the Admissions Office of a particular college or to contact that particular school to request one. There may be some schools that have printable applications on their websites as well. If you have selected this option, please complete the application in black ink. This is the preferred color choice for college and universities. Please refrain from using red ink or pencils when completing applications for admission. When submitting paper applications, use proper postage for each application that you send. You may want to invest in a book of postage stamps so that you will not have to make several trips to the post office. Lastly, you will want to check with each institution to ensure that they have received your application. There is nothing worse than assuming that your application materials have been received, when they have not. This way you can be certain all has been received and you can switch your focus on to the next steps.

Application Fees

Along with the wide variety of colleges and universities across the nation and abroad, there are also varying application fees. Application fees are included with most application requirements. There are some schools who do not charge application fees. If and when you find one of those schools bask in the savings. The average person spends about $40-$50 per application. That can become expensive if you are applying to ten or more schools. This is why it is suggested that you stick with, at most, five colleges. Application fees should be listed on the website where you find the application. If you have questions about the fees, pleased contact the institution where you are looking to apply. Most application fees are payable online with a credit or debit card. If you are submitting a paper application, check to see what the payment options are and if you can include a check or money order. Applications are not processed unless the application fee has been paid. If you have realized that you have submitted the application, and forgot your application fee, please get the application fee to the college as soon as you can.

Quick Check:

What is your application fee budget? _____

Application Fee Waiver

In the last section we mentioned that there are schools that do not require an application fee. These schools are rare so it is advisable to apply to the schools if they are on your list. There are also schools who offer application fee waivers. You will need to submit a form to waive the application fee for that school. Each school will have their own criteria that students will need to follow in order to receive a waiver approval. An example of specific application fee waiver criteria would be for low income students. Not all schools accept application waivers so please check to see if the school you are looking to apply to offer them.

Quick Check:

How many schools of interest offer application fee waivers? _____

Official Transcrits

Official transcripts are required by most colleges and universities in order to be considered for admission. Official transcripts are different from unofficial transcripts. The difference between official and unofficial transcripts is that official transcripts are in a sealed envelope. The seal is usually the school's seal. In the case that a student receives an official transcript, but they open the envelope before submitting to the college and universities, the transcripts at that point are considered unofficial. Official transcripts are best sent directly from the high school to the higher education institution. There are cases where an official transcript will be released to the student in a sealed envelope. The student then has options as to how he/she will submit those official transcripts to the college of their choice, which will be discussed in detail in the next section.

Mailed Transcripts .

There are two ways that colleges and universities can receive your official transcripts. The first of these options is via US mail. A student can have their high school mail their official transcripts directly to the prospective college. Make sure that when submitting the request for official transcripts that the school counselor, or whoever is sending the transcripts, knows the complete address where the transcripts need to be sent. If the address is incorrect, it could delay the time that it takes to receive and process your transcripts. Most colleges and universities list an exact address where all official documents can be shipped.

Another option is that students can mail the transcripts directly to the school themselves. If you choose to utilize this option, please make sure that the official documents are not tampered with and ensure that the seal is not broken. It is generally safer to put the official transcripts into another envelope to ensure that nothing happens to the transcripts while they are in transit to the intended college. As previously stated, make sure that the mailing address is correct before sending your transcript to avoid delivery delays.

ACTIVITY:
Purchase a book of stamps in preparation for mailing your own official transcripts.

Electronic Transcripts
The second way in which colleges receive official transcripts is electronically. Many high schools across the country have started to utilize the electronic option. This is a simple way to send and receive official transcripts. There are a couple of different electronic delivery services available. The two most commonly used services are Parchment and Naviance. Parchment has a relationship with over 3,000 high schools. They can electronically deliver official transcripts to over 2,000 institutions. With Parchment, schools can elect to send official transcripts electronically or via mail. The receiving institution can generally receive official transcripts faster if they are sent electronically. Another great thing to note about services like these is that you can track the transcripts from the time you place the order until it has been received. This is a good way to ensure that official transcripts have arrived to your institution. In the case that your

college of choice has not received transcripts that have been sent, it is likely that you can contact the high school to check the status of the transcripts. You can also obtain the transcript request order number from your high school and communicate to the college on your own.

ACTIVITY:

Speak with your high school counselor to find out if transcripts are electronically sent or if they are sent via US mail.

Essays

Essays are not required for entry into every college. The best way to find out if they are required is to look at the Admissions requirements for each of your selected colleges of interest. Essays give the Admissions committee additional insight into who you are as a student. It is best to write several sample essays during the summer of your junior year. Write on several topics due to the fact that some essays will be more about academic successes and others may explore out of school topics. Essay topics can range from a basic topic like "Why is this the right college for you?" to "Who is your hero and why?" Take a substantial amount of time gathering your thoughts with a clear and concise topic so that when the committee reads your essay they have no doubt in their minds that they need you on their campus. It is also highly recommended to allow a parent, English teacher, or Guidance Counselor to read your essay before submitting it. The more people that read your essays, the better they will be. There could be grammatical errors or tone agreement issues that you may have missed. It is suggested that students save their essays to a source they feel most comfortable with such as Google Docs, iCloud, a flash drive, etc. Whatever you do, do not just save the document on your computer without having a backup in case anything happens to your computer.

DYMENSIONS
Educational Consulting LLC

ACTIVITY:

What are some topics that you plan to write about in your essays?

_____

_____

_____

How many essays do you plan to compose? _____

Letters of Recommendation

Another component of the admissions process is letters of recommendation. As with most other criteria that has been mentioned so far, please check with your intended college to see if these are required before sending. Do not just assume that they are required. Some colleges want to hear how other people view you as a student, as an employee, or a volunteer. You should target anywhere from 3-5 people that you would like to ask if they would write a Letter of Recommendation on your behalf. Make sure that you have a favorable image in the eyes of the person you selected. Take some time to talk to those individuals personally. Tell them why you are interested in the specific schools that you are looking into. Inform them of the reasons that you selected your program of study. It would also be helpful to talk to them about your interests. You want these individuals to have a good idea of the type of person you are. Everyone that you ask may not agree to write a letter for you. That is why it is advised to have a list of five people just in case a person or two is unable to meet your request. In most cases, the people that you have selected can submit their letters via mail or email, depending on the requirements of the intended college or university.

ACTIVITY:

Name 3-5 people who know your work ethic and can attest to your good character.

    1. _____

    2. _____

    3. _____

    4. _____

    5. _____

Post Submission Possibility

Interview

You will find many admissions criteria throughout your application process. Many schools will have similar requirements, but there will be some that will be distinctive. One criterion is an interview. A selective group of schools are known for their interview requirements. An interview is a great opportunity to introduce yourself as a prospective student to their college. Much like a job interview, you will want to dress for success. Every high school senior should own basic black or grey slacks and a professional dress shirt. These would be ideal to wear should you be contacted for an interview at your Dream College or university. Before the interview, practice answering questions about yourself with your parents, friends, teachers, or mentors. Try to avoid phrases like: 'uh' or 'um'. If you forget your train of thought just pause, regroup, and continue on with your conversation. Be confident, but not overly confident. Be polite and respond verbally to questions rather than using non-verbal responses. Thoroughly research your school of choice so that you are knowledgeable about the different offerings and features of the school.

ACTIVITY:

Interview with a mentor, teacher, or professional to assist you in preparing for an interview if you are required to complete one. Make sure to research the college/university and know historical information.

Knowing and Understanding Deadlines

Earlier in this chapter, it was explained how important it is to not only compose a list of colleges and universities that you were interested in, but to also record application deadlines. Application deadlines are a very important part of this application process. Students should be aware of the dates that all application materials are due. The best way to avoid late submissions is to apply early. Some colleges and universities open applications two semesters before the first day of class. With that in mind, you want to be as prepared as possible. Request a copy of your unofficial transcripts prior to the end of your junior year. Use the transcript to complete your admissions applications. The longer you wait to submit your application materials, the more rushed and anxious you will feel. In order for this process to go smoothly

.everything should be completed in a timely fashion. Being prepared is one of the best assets anyone could ever have.

The Waiting Game

You have completed every task in the application process and now you are wondering what is next. Well, it is time to wait. If you followed the recommendations outlined in this chapter, you have applied early and you still have time to enjoy the rest of your summer. Take this opportunity to focus on the upcoming school year and to come up with a great game plan to finish out your high school experience. No matter how great you have done in the previous semester always remember one bad semester could jeopardize everything. Hopefully, when you submitted your application you were able to find the window of time that it will take before you hear back from your college of choice. It would be a good idea to color code the dates on your calendar so that you will know when to expect notification.

ACTIVITY:

Record two dates that you were given from colleges that you applied to in regards to notification of acceptance.

College Name: _____

Date #1: _____

Date #2: _____

Ensure That All Documents Have Been Received

Once you have submitted your application, it is important to check on your submission regularly. This is one of the most critical parts of the application process. Most colleges and universities have a checklist to assist students in staying informed of outstanding documents that need to be submitted. There will be time allotted to submit all documents throughout the application process. If you neglect to submit your documents in a timely fashion, your application will be marked incomplete. With an incomplete application, you cannot receive an admission decision. That is a sure way to miss out on the opportunity to attend one of the colleges on your list.

Confirmation Email

Once application materials have been received electronically, students should receive a confirmation email. The email should acknowledge the date and time of the submission. This will be useful if you have a delayed response and you want to ensure that the college or university has received your application. The email may inform you of an estimated of time that it should take to hear a response from the institution.

Attend On Campus Events

It is important to stay engaged with your colleges of choice. Once you complete your official list, you should start to visit those colleges. This is critical, even during the application process. You can visit the college's website to see if you can schedule a visit. Most sites will allow you to view availability for tours and other events happening on campus. Schools often host "Open House" events throughout the year so that prospective students have an opportunity to visit the schools. The academic resources should be explored as well. This includes the library, tutoring offices, and computer labs. It may also be a good idea to locate your potential advisor's office. Sporting events are always a great way to check out the campus as well. While on campus you should see if there is a way to tour your actual academic program facilities. This will give you a good perspective on where you will spend most of your time as a student. Another great idea is to see if your future department offers workshops for your intended major. Attending workshops is an excellent way to become acclimated with the institution.

ACTIVITY:

Plan a campus visit and write about your experience. Compose a paragraph or two regarding your on campus experience. What was your favorite part? Did you go on a tour? If you did, can you see yourself fitting in on campus?

_____

_____

_____

_____

_____

_____

_____

_____

_____

_____

_____

_____

_____

_____

DYMENSIONS
Educational Consulting LLC

Continue Applying For Scholarships

The application has been submitted and you have visited the campus. During the waiting stage, you still should have plenty of time to apply for scholarships. You do not need to wait until the middle of your senior year to apply for scholarships. It is important to start the scholarship process as early as possible. There are many other students who will be competing with you for the scholarships that you are interested in obtaining. College tuition is rising every year and it seems the more tuition goes up, the more difficult it is to afford it. In order to be prepared for the scholarship application deadlines, you must make sure that you are being proactive and prepared. If you need further assistance with completing scholarship applications, please seek assistance from your high school counselor, a mentor, or a qualified college consultant as soon as possible. Check out chapter 5 to learn more about scholarships.

ACTIVITY:

List the names of 3 scholarships that you plan to apply for.

1. _____

2. _____

3. _____

I'm IN….

You checked the mail today and your letter of acceptance has finally arrived. You have been admitted into your top pick college. CONGRATULATIONS! All of your hard work has paid off. You can now celebrate. You have been waiting for weeks for this moment and it's finally here. Quick, call your family and friends and let them know the good news. Hopefully, this is the first of a line of other acceptance letters.

ACTIVITY:

List the colleges/universities that you have been admitted to.

1. _____

2. _____

3. _____

4. _____

5. _____

Decide Which College/University Is Best Suited For You

You have now heard back from all of your colleges and universities, but now you are faced with making a tough decision. For the past couple of months, you have been trying to prove to colleges and universities why you belong at their institutions, now it is your time to make a choice. Selecting the right school for you can be a difficult task. It can take some time for you to make this decision if you are approaching it the right way. You must begin by thinking about what you want for yourself in the future. Think about how you would like to live as an adult. This decision will affect your future so be sure to make it count. When going through this process you should be considering various parts of the college life at each institution. You should consider your intended program major and how it compares to the colleges that have accepted you. A major factor for most people is cost. How do these schools compare? When going through the selection phase, it's much like shopping for clothes. You have to figure out which college fits your needs and personality the best. As previously mentioned, this process might be a little tough, but once you start asking yourself some of the above questions, it will make it much easier.

Confirm Your Admissions with First Choice College/University

It is time to settle the infamous question of "which school did you choose?". You have already weighed all of your options, and the positives and negatives of attending each institution that accepted you. Now, you have confidently selected the school that you feel will put you on your path to success. It is time to inform the school that you plan to attend. Although this stage may be similar for most colleges and universities, you should follow the specific instructions provided in your acceptance letters so that you can properly confirm that you plan to attend the college of your choice.

ACTIVITY:

Which college/university did you select? And why did you select this particular college/university?

_____

_____

_____

_____

_____

Find Out Next Steps

As mentioned before, every institution will have their own confirmation process as well as specific steps that should be taken for each newly admitted student. If you have any questions about next steps for any given institution, please reach out to your Admissions Counselor.

Select Orientation Date

Depending on your new college or university, you will most likely need to set up an orientation date. Orientation for freshman students, is generally two days long, so expect to spend the night on campus. Orientations are usually family friendly, which means that students can attend with their parents. Before making plans for your family to attend, please contact the intended college to confirm. Orientation will be your first official experience as a freshman on campus. This is the time where you will be introduced to a wide variety of college-specific information. You can begin to locate certain campus resources and most of all, and you can start making friends. Orientation days follow a standard, tight timeline of scheduled events. There may or may not be fees associated with Orientation, so be sure to have clarity on that before moving forward.

ACTIVITY:

When is Orientation scheduled? _____

Select Housing Options

It is now time to set your sights on where you will live while on campus. Hopefully, by this point you have toured the campus to see all that it has to offer. One of the biggest decisions is where you will live. Some colleges have specific residence halls that freshman are confined to while some colleges have no specific housing parameters for freshman to follow. It is up to you decide which residence would be a good fit. Also, it should be noted that in most cases, housing deposits will be required to hold a spot in a residence hall.

ACTIVITY:

Where did you decide to reside during the school year?

_____

_____

_____

I'm OUT...

You have been waiting the moment where you could hold the institution envelope in your hand. You examine the envelope to test how thick it is hoping that this will provide you with a clue of the contents of the envelope. You quickly tear the envelope open while holding your breath searching for those infamous letters that spell 'CONGRATULATIONS'. Instead you read the words "Unfortunately we regret to inform you….." It feels bad to read those words. You may be devastated; you may have been caught off guard. Just know that this does not define your destiny. Everyone will not get the news that they were hoping for. There are a number of reasons why a student would not be admitted into the college or university of their choice. In life, you will learn that several no's come before a single 'yes'. Most successful people will tell you this. Success does not come without a few bumps along the road. These bumps should push you to be a greater version of yourself.

Appeal Process

In most cases, it is unlikely that a student would be able to appeal a decision that was rendered by their college or university of choice. There are a few schools that may consider an appeal, but only if there are substantial changes in the documents that the committee reviewed. Some colleges have very complicated procedures when it comes to admissions so rescinding a decision most times is not possible. The appeal process can give you a second chance to be deemed as admissible at your prospective college. The very first thing to do is to review your rejection letter to see why you were not accepted into the college of choice. Once you have a clear understanding as to why you were denied admission, you should create a letter that addresses those particulars. This would be extremely useful if you're GPA or your ACT score has increased. Maybe you had an extreme situation taking place while you were in school that may have prohibited you from doing well. This letter is a good place to include such issues. The appeal process may also include Letters of Recommendation. Just remember that each institution has their own rules and may handle situations like these differently.

Resubmit GPA (After Current Semester)

As previously discussed, there are some colleges and universities that have an appeal process. If appealing is a possibility, you may be able to resubmit your GPA. Now, understand that if you submitted your original application with a 2.5 GPA and now you have a 2.57 and the school requires a minimum 2.8, appealing may not be the best process for you. This is why it is pivotal to know and understand exactly what the school is looking for from other applicants. If you had a 2.5 and somehow your GPA reached that 2.8, then appealing the decision may be an option. You should do everything you can to show the institution how dedicated and how serious you are about your education.

Resubmit ACT/SAT Scores

Another appeal option that may assist you is to resubmit your ACT or SAT scores. Again, if the appeal process is an option for your institution, consider re-taking the ACT and/or the SAT for a better score. Once you receive your new scores, you may want to have them sent directly to the college or university that you are looking to be accepted by. Similar to the previous section, if you saw growth in your scores that could possibly gain you admission to your dream school, go for it. If that does not happen, there are always other avenues to research: such as trade schools or community colleges.

FINISH STRONG

The last semester of high school has finally arrived. You have just about made it through your last year of high school. It should be noted that you must continue to stay focused on academics until the very last day of school. Make sure that you have kept your school behavior in tact as to avoid any last-minute changes to your admission decision with the college/university of choice. Take some time to reflect on all of the experiences that you embarked upon in high school. Think about the teachers who made such a great impact on your high school career. Reflect on the first time you stepped into the school and thought how huge it was and how you thought you would never figure out how to make it to your first class. Do not forget to think about your friends and how they have played such an intricate part of your high school years. Lastly, finish strong! Leave a lasting impact on your academic record at your high school.

Submit Final HS Transcripts

Now that you have graduated, in some cases colleges may want to see your final high school transcript. This transcript should include all of your grades from 9th grade through 12th grade. You want to ensure that they have everything that they need from you. Never be afraid to ask if there is anything additional that you need to submit. It is always good to stay on top of your 'to do list". Hopefully you have created a "to do list" that would have included the many processes that you have completed throughout this chapter. Lastly, note that during the summer, high schools may not be fully staffed so please keep that in mind when you need documents after school has ended for the year.

Enjoy Your Summer with Family & Friends

YOU MADE IT!!! It is now summer time. You were prepared and now you can spend your time relaxing with family and friends. As stated earlier, preparation is the key to life. Do everything within your power to keep that at the forefront of your mind. Never allow time to get the best of you. Stay ahead when it comes to deadlines. Find out what the best strategies are to approach life's situations and move forward. All of the hard work that you have done to prepare yourself for college will be utilized while you are in college. The only difference is that your parents may or may not be there physically, with the guidance that they were able to give while you were in high school. When you enter college, you will experience a new world. Rules will be different; you will see things that you may have never seen and experience things that you may have never experienced, but always stay true to who you are. Take this summer to relax. Pat yourself on the back for a job well done. Good luck and stay focused!!!

ACTIVITY:

Name 3 activities that you plan to do with family and friends this summer.

_____

_____

_____

_____

_____

_____

DYMENSIONS
Educational Consulting LLC

Chapter 5:   SCHOLARSHIPS AND FINANCIAL AID

Scholarships:

Scholarships are not just about completing an application, writing an essay, or submitting your GPA to get money for college. When a person or organization is seeking students to give scholarships to, they want to know your potential for success. They want to know who you are. What you have accomplished and if you are the best person to represent their organization when giving away their money. Applying for scholarships is like a competition. In order to compete, you have to know what you bring to the table and how to present it.

Applying for scholarships is also like applying for college admission or even a job. You must go through the process and just like applying for a job or college admission; each one will have different requirements. It is important to make sure you complete each step in the process. Presentation is everything.

Believe it or not, presentation can be a determining factor in whether or not you get the scholarship. Some things that make up your presentation for a scholarship are spelling, punctuation, and grammar, descriptive language, meeting timelines, cleanliness of paper, proper formatting, and sequence of events in your essay. You may want to consider applying for scholarships that are geared towards all groups or criteria. Selecting scholarships solely on merit may not be enough. Think outside the box when selecting and applying for scholarships. You may find that you can apply for many scholarships that are available.

Assignment:

Identify a person, parent, teacher, or counselor who can proofread and review all of your scholarship applications. Let them know you will be applying for some scholarships and ask if they would agree to proof and edit your applications and essays. If they aren't comfortable, ask if they can recommend someone.

How Much Will College Cost?

College will be one of the largest investments you can make. College will cost you money and time, none of which you can get back, so invest wisely. What you are doing now? You are taking time to read this book. It is a small price to pay as opposed to attending college.

Before you start your scholarship search and completing applications, you need to at least have an idea of how much you will need so you can determine how much to apply for in scholarships. The amount you need for college will depend on several factors; where you go to school (in State vs. out of state), what type of school (private or public), what type of major (some courses require additional fees), and how long it will take you to finish, 2 years, 4 years, 5 years or longer. Most importantly, where you get scholarship, financial aid, student loans or grants. All of these factors play a major part when it comes to estimating the cost of college; in addition to the fact that college tuition generally goes up each year. To help you identify how much you will need for college, here are some of the things you need to take time to research.

ASSIGNMENT:

Create an excel spreadsheet and factor in the following: School (in State vs out of State), tuition and extra class fee, room and board (or dorm room), accessories (printer, cable, TV), bedding and toiletries, meal plan, and extra-curricular activities.

Who Are You?

We previously talked about presentation and how important it is when applying for scholarships. One of the major things you will present in a scholarship essay is WHO YOU ARE. To receive a scholarship, you have to clearly identify Who You Are, your accomplishments and experiences, what make you the best candidate and why you deserve to win the scholarship money.

You can use the academic profile that you created at the beginning of this book to identify yourself. It is also important to write a personal statement. This should include goals that you plan to accomplish.

To help with writing your essays for scholarships, be prepared to write on these topics:

A personal experience and what you learned from it.

What is your leadership experience?

Create a short story telling about yourself.

What are your plans after high school?

How will a scholarship help you achieve your goals?

DYMENSIONS
Educational Consulting LLC

ASSIGNMENT:

Create your personal statement: include a unique fact about you, summarize accomplishments, and add your professional goal.

Personal Statement

_____

_____

_____

_____

_____

_____

_____

_____

_____

_____

_____

_____

_____

_____

_____

_____

_____

_____

_____

_____

How to make a Standout Presentation

In this chapter, we talked about your presentation on paper when completing a scholarship application. Understand, your presentation can go beyond the essay.

As technology expands and competition for scholarships becomes more in depth, some scholarships may require face to face interviews or they may look at your social media page to see if you are the person you portray on paper. Gone are the days when you go to an interview in a dark blue, black, or brown suit. Interviewers are more interested in if what you are wearing is well put together. A simple accessory stands out but does not overpower the outfit. For ladies, natural look in make-up, ladies and gentlemen your hair is well groomed or does your personality show in your clothes while keeping it professional.

Social Media: When applying for scholarships, internships or jobs, your social media page can be reviewed. If you currently have Facebook, Instagram, Twitter, etc., any posts on your page that are risky, close it, a little risky, close it, delete it and start over. Be intentional about what you post, what you share, or what you allow others to post on your page. Guilt by association can cost you. Make sure what you post on your social media represents you and how you want to be seen by someone making the final decision on your scholarship application and that it is consistent with what you say in your interview. Create a theme around your social media if you are an athlete, in music, or arts, etc. Create a header and Professional Profile picture that represents your interests. Creating posts and pictures to show your interest is okay or showing pictures of you having fun celebrating an achievement with your team. Making a "Stand Out" presentation is all about you, your uniqueness, and what makes you different yet qualified. It is about being intentional when you show up in person, on paper, or on social media. It is about branding yourself with a certain color, style, or trade that will make someone remember you. You were not created to fit in you were created to stand out.

DYMENSIONS
Educational Consulting LLC

ACTIVITY:

What do you want to be known for; academics, athlete, music, arts, dance, theatre, technology person, foreign languages, science, or math?

1. Create a picture that speaks to who you are.

2. Create a social banner that represents how you want people to see you.

3. Create two to three professional outfits with an accessory or color that brings out your personality but not too much.

4. List three things about you: achievements, experience or character traits that make you different or that you think makes you stand out.

Creating a System to Master your Scholarship Search.

Many people realize the scholarship process is not as easy as it sounds and give up quickly. Like anything, it gets easier with practice and a system. Before you go on a frantic search, take time to organize a system that fits your needs. Identify all the things that are important to you when looking at schools, and be realistic about what you and your parents can afford.

Search for scholarships based on your age, nationality, or special interest. Search for scholarships offered by organizations or companies, local and national. There are a lot of scholarship sites, so you will spend most of your time doing research. Remember, as you find scholarships you qualify for, enter them into a spreadsheet and set a time to come back to them. Do not try to research and complete scholarships at the same time, this can be overwhelming. Set time aside each day or week to research scholarships and set time aside each day or week to apply for scholarships.

Time management is the key to mastering your scholarship search. Creating a system for certain scholarships and completing the system can make the process easier and doable. Creating a spreadsheet is an easy way to creating your system.

ACTIVITY:

Spreadsheet #1

Use the spreadsheet below to answer the following questions.

1. List the schools that you are interested in attending and make sure that these schools have the program you are interested in.

2. How much is the school going to cost yearly to attend including room, board, and fees?

3. Set a goal of how much money you want to receive in scholarships that are not awarded by the school.

Schools	Cost of Attendance	Scholarship Awards

DYMENSIONS
Educational Consulting LLC

Spreadsheet #2

Use the spreadsheet below to answer the following questions.

1. List the names of the scholarships you are applying for

2. Add the link to these scholarships

3. How much is the scholarship awarding?

4. Is the process an application or an essay?

5. What is the due date?

Scholarship Name	Application Link	Scholarship Amount	Type of Application	Scholarship Due Date

DYMENSIONS
Educational Consulting LLC

Some things to remember about scholarship search:

1. It takes an investment of time to research and complete applications.

2. You may not receive the first scholarship. Do not get discouraged. Keep applying.

3. Be prepared to complete at least 100 scholarship applications or more to get the money.

Financial Aid

The Department of Education is responsible for grants and loans that are offered to students working toward a higher education degree. Students must apply for Financial Aid using the Federal Student Aid application. (See website/reference page) This is a free application. It is very important that you avoid using any websites that request payment for FAFSA completion.

Grants

Federal grants are financial aid awards that do not have to be repaid. They are awarded to students based on financial need and enrollment status into a college or university. Completing the FAFSA will determine your eligibility. Grants can be used to cover tuition expenses such as room and board, tuition, books and other enrollment related fees.

Pell Grant

Federal Pell Grants are awarded only to undergraduate students who have not earned a bachelor's or a professional degree.

The amount you get will depend on:

- *financial need,*
- cost of attendance,
- status as a full-time or part-time student, and
- plans to attend school for a full *academic year* or less.

Note: You may not receive Federal Pell Grant funds from more than one school at a time.

Federal Supplemental Educational Opportunity Grant (FSEOG).

The FSEOG program is administered directly by the *financial aid office* at participating schools (Not all schools participate).

You can receive between $100 and $4,000 a year, depending on your financial need. Each participating school receives a certain amount of FSEOG funds each year from the Department of Education's office of Federal Student Aid. Once the full amount of the school's FSEOG funds has been awarded to students, no more FSEOG awards can be made for that year.

You must maintain enrollment as an undergraduate student and must not have previously earned a bachelor's degree. Your eligibility for the FSEOG is determined by **completing the FAFSA form** on an annual basis. Your institution will award the FSEOG each year based on that eligibility and other factors at the college.

Loans

Student loans consist of money borrowed from the Department of Education for tuition cost. In order to determine if you are eligible for borrowing, you must complete the *Free Application for Federal Student Aid application.* This is an application that must be completed every year that you are enrolled in a college or university. If you qualify for financial aid, you can borrow **$5,500** to **$12,500** per year. Loan limits are determined by your status as an independent student or still claimed as a dependent by your parents.

Direct Subsidized Loans:

- Available to undergraduate students with financial need.
- College or University determines the amount you can borrow, and the amount may not exceed your financial need.
- The U.S. Department of Education pays the interest on a Direct Subsidized Loan
  - While you're in school at least half-time.
  - For the first six months after you leave school. (referred to as a *grace period**)

o   During a period of *deferment* (a postponement of loan payments).

Direct Unsubsidized Loans:

- Are available to undergraduate and graduate students; there is no requirement to demonstrate financial need.

- Amount borrowed is based on your cost of attendance and other financial aid you receive.

- You are responsible for paying interest on Direct Unsubsidized Loan during all periods.

- If you choose not to pay the interest while you are in school and during grace periods and deferment or *forbearance* periods, your interest will accrue (accumulate) and be capitalized (that is, your interest will be added to the principal amount of your loan).

Once your financial aid has been awarded, you must complete Entrance/exit Counseling and sign a Master Promissory Note. This process can be completed on the Student Loans website. (See website/reference page)

Financial aid (loans/grants) can cover:

Tuition is the cost of your academic classes.

Fees are charged by colleges/universities for general expenses, such as technology and activities.

Room and Board is the cost of a place to live (room) and your meals (board)

Transportation is the cost of trips home during the holidays; if you commute from home every day, this is the cost of getting to class and back home.

Other Expenses include books, living expenses and spending money.

Let's do some research. Fill in the cost of attendance for three schools of your choice.

School #1		
Tuition		
Room and Board		
Books and Supplies		
Health Insurance		
Personal Expenses		
Transportation		

School #2		
Tuition		
Room and Board		
Books and Supplies		
Health Insurance		
Personal Expenses		
Transportation		

School #3		
Tuition		
Room and Board		
Books and Supplies		
Health Insurance		
Personal Expenses		
Transportation		

Chapter 6: CAREER PLANNING

As you continue to navigate through your college years, you have an important task to complete which will have a major impact on your future. The daunting task of deciding what career path you will choose to devote the remainder of your adult life to can be a significant milestone at this juncture. By this time, you may have had work and extra-curricular experiences, both inside and outside of school that could have an influence on your future career choice. There are also other outside factors that could contribute to your decision making process that could include personality traits, strengths, interests, and hobbies. Throughout this chapter, you will explore various aspects of your personal, professional life, and experiences in order to discover a career path that would be the best fit for you.

Self-Assessment: Getting to Know Yourself

Interests

One of the first steps to making a decision regarding your career path is to gain a better understanding of who you are and what interests you. You want to begin by thinking about what types of tasks or duties you are most interested in. Are you interested in working with your hands, helping others, or utilizing technology? Would you say that you like to build or design things or would you rather work with or care for others? The next aspect would be to take a closer look at your personality traits.

Would you describe yourself as being self-motivated, creative, athletic, or a lover of nature? Are you good at solving problems, inquisitive, or innovative? Another important area to consider is the type of courses that you have or are currently taking in high school. Perhaps there is a particular subject that interests you. For instance, do you get excited about solving algebraic expressions or do you enjoy learning about historical events? These are all things that could help determine what types of jobs or careers that would suit you best.

Activity:

1.) Complete the O*NET *Interest Profiler Short Form* found (see website/reference page)
2.) Follow the on-screen directions and complete the 60 question profiler. Record your results from each

of the interest categories (RIASEC):

Interest	Score
Realistic	
Investigative	
Artistic	
Social	
Enterprising	
Conventional	

3.) Next, choose the job zone that closely matches the type of career you would like to have in the future.

Be sure to read the descriptions of each of the five job zones as they provide the type of experience,

education, and training that is needed for jobs. Each job zone also provides examples of jobs that would

match specific criteria.

Chosen Job Zone: _____

After completing the steps of the interest profiler, list your top three career fields that would best match

your personal interests and preparation level.

1. _____

2. _____

3. _____

Now that you have completed the Interest Profiler, you should have a better idea of the type of work that you most enjoy based on your current interests. The next area to take a look at would be your current hobbies, extra-curricular activities, or past times that you engage in both inside and outside of school. The types of activities that you are involved in could help you to make connections to the skills that you use in these activities and skills. This is important for specific careers of interest. When considering the activities, think about the types of skills that are required to successfully perform the various tasks. The skills that you use can then transfer to future job functions. Regardless of the types of hobbies or activities that you enjoy, there are varying correlations amongst them and the different types of jobs that you can have. Perhaps you are an athlete in school; there are a number of job related skills that you can learn when playing a sport. A few of these skills include responsibility, leadership qualities, working with a team, and following the directives of the team captain or coach. These are all significant skills that would be important to have when working. Another example would be someone who enjoys scrapbooking. This type of activity would also provide one with skills that could be transferred to a future career such as organization, creativity, and appreciation for the arts, to name a few.

Activity:
Create a list of hobbies, extra-curricular activities, or past times that you are involved in and describe the corresponding skills that you have developed as a result.

Activity	Skill(s)

Personal Skills and Strengths

One of the things that many people struggle with is acknowledging their own personal strengths and abilities as it relates to various aspects of our lives. We can, oftentimes, be overcritical of ourselves and have difficulty accepting praise and positive acknowledgements. When making a decision about what would be the best career choice for you, it would be important to gain a better appreciation for your own personal strengths and skills. One way to do this would be to examine some of the different components of your life that provide outlets for feedback and/or criticism. Examples of this would be school, job experiences, and extra-curricular activities (discussed in the last section). Thinking back across the span of your school career, what were some of your major accomplishments? Did you earn any type of rewards or recognition because of something that you excelled in? Were you ever recognized by an adult or another peer for something that you did? It can be assumed that, along with this recognition, there was something that you had to have done prior to receiving such praise and acknowledgement.

Activity:

List 3 – 5 personal or professional accomplishments that you have had over the past 10 years.

_____

_____

_____

_____

_____

DYMENSIONS
Educational Consulting LLC

After creating your list, reflect on these accomplishments and describe the skills that emerged as a result.

_____

_____

_____

_____

_____

_____

Transferrable Competencies

In addition to the skills that have earned you recognition, there are other skills that you may possess that could make you a valuable asset to a company or specific profession. These skills are known as *transferable competencies or skills*. The National Research Council (2013) describes transferrable competencies or skills as those that are often developed or learned in a specific context (i.e. classroom/school environment or other jobs) that can be utilized in another setting. Examples of transferrable skills include problem solving and analytical skills, communication, people management, and the ability to think creatively. These are the types of skills that future employers also value in addition to looking at your experiences, activities, and transcripts. Furthermore, these skills are important to include in your resume in order to help support your candidacy for the position. So when reflecting on your transferrable skills, the first thing that you want to ask yourself is, "What am I good at?" What can I bring to the table that would make me a valuable asset to a company? Your responses to these questions are important because this will be another way to market yourself for the career of your dreams.

DYMENSIONS
Educational Consulting LLC

Activity:

Identify at least 5 transferrable skills that you possess and explain how they would make you a valuable asset to a company or profession.

_____

_____

_____

_____

_____

_____

_____

_____

_____

_____

_____

_____

_____

_____

_____

_____

Values and Ethics:

The next major area of focus would be to survey your personal work ethic and values. The reason that this is so important is because there may be careers that exist that do not align with your personal beliefs or values. Perhaps you have started to recognize that there are specific things that you require when working with others. Even though you have had no prior work experiences, there are values that you have that may be inherent to you. This means that there are values that you may have obtained from your parents or other family member. You have even recognized some qualities from your current teachers or coaches at school. Some examples could include specific working demands, the types of job tasks and responsibilities that are required, or the specific expectations that are required of all employees. Although you may be qualified and capable, there may be jobs that you may not be comfortable with doing or careers that may not align with your specific lifestyle or personality. When thinking about your work ethic, what are some things that you have already begun to recognize are important to you when placed in a work environment? For example, do you value a workplace that is open to input for everyone? One that values the importance of each individual that is employed at the workplace? One that will allow active participation and input from all employees? Do you prefer a work environment that is positive and uplifting, one that promotes shared decision-making, and provides opportunities for growth? Maybe you require a work setting that is flexible, one that acknowledges scheduling differences, or one that is a non-traditional work environment. Do you value a work environment that sends the message of trust and equal responsibility, where one is praised and acknowledged often for the hard work they are doing for the organization?

Activity:

Think about your personal work ethic or values. What would be important values that you would want to see at your future workplace or within your future career?

_____

_____

_____

_____

Career Exploration

You have just gone through a journey of self-investigation. You should have been able to identify your strengths, skill set, work values and ethics, and the different career fields that would be most appropriate for you based on your interests and personality. So now what do you do? The next step would be to analyze all of the information you obtain from the first part of this chapter. Use it to identify what type of careers you would be most interested in, as well as careers that would be a good fit for you. The focus for this section is to take your research a step further and begin to explore career options. At first, the process for planning for a career at this stage in your academic development may seem overwhelming or far-fetched. In actuality, this is the best time to begin engaging in this exploration process. It will give you more information to help you make decisions when planning for college. Having an idea of the type of career you want when you leave college will assist you with planning the courses that you will take, the types of activities that you become involved with, and the types of training you will need. The information you obtained may even suggest a particular type of college or university that you should attend based on your interests and needs. For example, if one of your career paths includes working with marine life, it would benefit you to attend a school that specializes in that field. The other thing to be aware of is that things may change for you by the time you graduate from high school. There may be new interests and activities that you gain. This may impact your selection of careers in the future.

The next activity in this chapter will involve conducting research on three careers of interest that you have identified; utilizing the information from previous sections of this chapter. The ultimate goal of this activity is to provide a comparison of multiple career choices that you can have based on your interests, strengths, and values. It will also help you to gain a better understanding of the requirements (i.e. previous experiences, type of degree, and schooling) that are necessary to work in particular fields. Lastly, you will get a full picture of the earning potential and opportunities for growth in the field for all three career choices.

Activity:

- Go to the Bureau of Labor Statistics' website.

- Select three different careers of interest to research.

- Complete the worksheets on the following page, one for each career that you research.

Career Planning Worksheet

Career One: _____

What do people in this career field do? (Describe at least three specific job tasks.)

_____

_____

What are the working conditions that one would experience in this career? (i.e. work hours, travel expectations, attire, etc.)

_____

_____

What is the median (average) salary for this career? (If not salaried, how much earnings per hour?)

_____

What is the career growth rate (percent)? _____

What college degree or training would be required for this career? (i.e. HS Diploma, Bachelor's degree, licensure or certification, etc.)

_____

_____

How many years of college or training would be required?

_____

Based on the information you obtained from the self-assessment portion of this chapter, identify three transferrable skills that would help you to be successful at this career.

_____

_____

_____

What current activities or hobbies are you involved in that will help you to continue to develop skills that are important for this career?

_____

_____

Career Planning Worksheet

Career Two: _____

What do people in this career field do? (Describe at least three specific job tasks.)

_____

_____

What are the typical working conditions that one would experience in this career? (i.e. work hours, travel expectations, attire, etc.)

_____

_____

What is the median (average) salary for this career? (If not salaried, how much earning per hour?)

_____

What is the career growth rate (percent)? _____

What college degree or training would be required for this career? (i.e. HS Diploma, Bachelor's degree, licensure or certification, etc.)

_____

_____

How many years of college or training would be required?

_____

Based on the information you obtained from the self-assessment portion of this chapter, identify three transferrable skills that would help you to be successful at this career.

_____

_____

_____

What current activities or hobbies are you involved in that will help you to continue to develop skills that are important for this career?

_____

_____

DYMENSIONS
Educational Consulting LLC

Career Planning Worksheet

Career Three: _____

What do people in this career field do? (Describe at least three specific job tasks.)

_____

_____

What are the typical working conditions that one would experience in this career? (i.e. work hours, travel expectations, attire, etc.)

_____

_____

What is the median (average) salary for this career? (If not salaried, how much earning per hour?)

_____

What is the career growth rate (percent)? _____

What college degree or training would be required for this career? (i.e. HS Diploma, Bachelor's degree, licensure or certification, etc.)

_____

_____

How many years of college or training would be required?

_____

Based on the information you obtained from the self-assessment portion of this chapter, identify three transferrable skills that would help you to be successful at this career.

_____

_____

_____

What current activities or hobbies are you involved in that will help you to continue to develop skills that are important for this career?

_____

_____

DYMENSIONS
Educational Consulting LLC

Now that you have completed that process, you should have three snapshots of careers that would be a good fit for you. This is based on your identified interests, skills, and strengths. By completing the research on these careers, you should have been able to recognize some notable positives and negatives of each of the careers. Perhaps you were not thrilled with the earning potential for that particular career or you were not looking forward to going beyond a two- or four-year degree program. One of the other important factors that you were researching was the growth rate for that particular career. This is important because the career that you choose will have long term impacts on your life. When researching careers on the Bureau of Labor Statistics' website, you may have come across a table that showed the job growth projections for certain careers over the next 10 years. Other features that may stand out when conducting the career research were the typical functions of people who hold these careers as well as the types of working conditions to which they are. These are also important aspects to take into consideration when determining your career path.

Activity:

After analyzing the research that you collected from the career planning worksheets, select your top career choice of the three. This is the career that will be used to complete the remaining activities in this chapter.

Top Career Choice: _____

What are three key features of this career that appealed most to you and why?

_____

_____

_____

Job Search Tools

One of the most challenging tasks involved with career planning is trying to find the perfect job within your career field. It can be very difficult for students who are approaching their college graduation (and new graduates) to land that dream job right away. There are a number of graduates who find themselves unemployed post-graduation who are experiencing significant challenges with finding a position worthy of their expensive degree. When talking to many people who are in this situation, it is immediately apparent that they may not have been provided with the tools to adequately search for career opportunities upon graduation. In addition to working with your college or university's Career Center (discussed later in this chapter), there are a number of job search engines that offer a wealth of information and job postings. Most of these engines have filtering abilities that allow you to identify the career field, location, and level of education and/or experience (i.e., entry-level, mid-level, executive level, etc.). Furthermore, the job search tools will often provide ways to create an online account and upload your resume or other supporting employment documents which makes it much easier to apply for jobs directly from the search engine sites. An additional aspect of job search tools is that there are search engines that are geared towards specific career fields.

Activity:

Based on the career choice that you identified as the top choice of the three you researched, find 3 different job search resources or tools that have postings related to that specific career. (If you are having difficulty locating a resource or tool specific to your career choice, list the filter options that you would use on a generalized job search site to locate vacant positions in that field.)

_____

_____

_____

College Connections

What an exciting, yet potentially stressful time in your lives as you have a number of major decisions to make. Don't worry; it is only preparing you for adulthood! In the "Choosing the Right College" chapter, you should have explored a few colleges or universities that you would be interested in attending post-graduation from high school. Hopefully, when selecting your top choices, you had some idea of the type of career you would be interested in having and had that in mind during that process. One of the most overlooked aspects of colleges and universities is the number of career planning resources that they have for students to utilize during and after attendance. Many students do not begin their freshman year of college with a solid idea of what road they may travel after graduating. Freshman year is all about experiencing the college life, making new friends, and getting a taste of freedom. It is typical, at this stage, for colleges and universities to host information sessions and orientations for incoming freshman. They will embed career planning information into a presentation that most freshman will ignore as it, unknowingly, bears no relevance to them at this point in their college journey. However, this is absolutely not the case and college students should be exposed to these resources at a very early stage of their college careers. The next activity will help you to explore one of your top college or universities websites to obtain further information related to some of the resources they offer for students with regard to career planning and development.

Activity: Complete the College Resources worksheet

College Resources

College or University: _____

Web Address: _____

I. Based on your top career choice, research the school's website to find information on student groups and activities on campus that could enhance your personal skills for that career.

<table>
<tr><th>Student Group/Activity</th><th>Skill Enhancements</th></tr>
<tr><td>_____</td><td>_____</td></tr>
<tr><td>_____</td><td>_____</td></tr>
<tr><td>_____</td><td>_____</td></tr>
<tr><td>_____</td><td>_____</td></tr>
<tr><td>_____</td><td>_____</td></tr>
<tr><td>_____</td><td>_____</td></tr>
</table>

II. Locate the career center website for this college or university. Describe the types of tools and resources available for students related to career planning.

Web Address: _____

_____

_____

_____

_____

_____

_____

_____

III. In your opinion, how easy was it to navigate through the career center? How helpful were the resources and tools?

_____

_____

DYMENSIONS
Educational Consulting LLC

Career Goal Setting

Goal setting is an extremely important part of successful career planning. It can be difficult to visualize the things that you need to do in order to get to where you want to be in life. In many cases, nothing will be handed to you. You will have to put in hard work and effort to achieve the things you want to accomplish. Many adults have struggled with goal setting because it can be hard to see what steps you need to complete before getting to the finish line. The easiest part is being able to describe the end goal, but what will it actually take to get there? With many professionals, be it athletes, doctors, lawyers, or teachers, they did not just wake up and become these things, they had to put in work to get there. So what will it take for you to get to the career of your dreams? How much work, effort, and schooling will it take for you to get there? In order to get a general idea of your journey and what it will take for you to get to your dream job, we need to be able to visualize it.

Roadmap to Success

Reflecting on all the information that you have gathered about yourself and your ideal career, you should be able to begin to see how some of the pieces will need to fit together. The next activity will involve you creating a tentative Roadmap to Success. This will be a visual representation of the steps you will need to take to get to your end goal. Within this roadmap, you will want to include things that you foresee to be potential stops, roadblocks, and/or detours along your journey. Keep in mind that this is a tentative roadmap and could change as you go on to experience life. Starting with an idea of what it will look like will be helpful when looking ahead.

Activity:

Complete the Roadmap to Success activity. Include the various steps that you think it will take you to get to your career goal. (Roadmap located on page **118**)

The Long and Short of It

In addition to creating the roadmap to success, it is important to set goals along the way that will assist you with reaching your ultimate career goal. Goal setting is key to being able to visualize and make your objective be clearer. Goals will help to keep you motivated to stay on track and to give you something to keep pushing forward. When developing goals for yourself, you want to make sure they are specific to your particular needs and are able to be measured. You also want to make sure that they are realistic goals, things that you are able to actually attain in the designated amount of time. For example, it is not realistic for you to go straight from high school right into a career as a nurse. You will need to take other steps in between to get you to that point prior to being able to be successful at that career. Lastly, the goals that you set must have a specific time limit associated with them. For a short term goal to be short, you want to set a realistic timeline for completion. In theory, it would be sufficient to expect that a short-term goal would be one that would be achieved within a year. Long-term goals, in essence, would then be a goal that would take you longer than a year to achieve. After you create these goals, you can refer back to them, at any time, to get back focused and reenergized to carry on.

Activity:

Develop two short term goals and two long term goals that you will set for yourself to help you reach your career goal.

Short-term goal #1:

_____

_____

_____

Short-term goal #2:

_____

_____

Long-term goal #1:

_____

_____

_____

Long-term goal #2:

_____

_____

_____

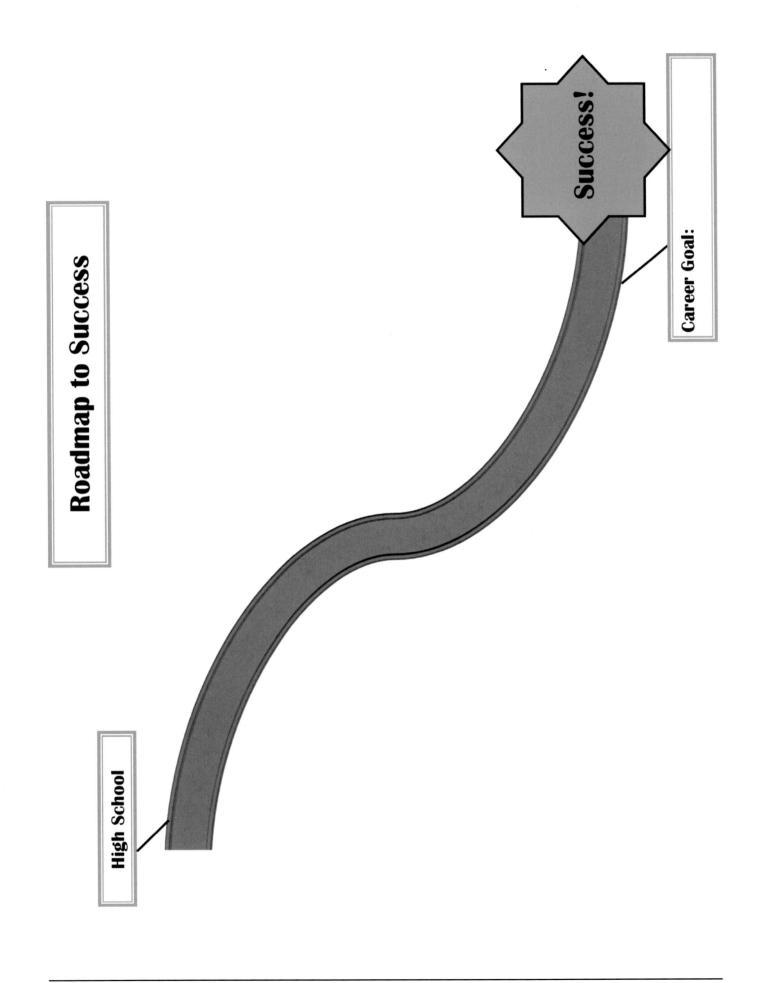

Roadmap to Success

High School

Career Goal:

Success!

APPENDIX A
References

BUREAU, O. L. S. (2015). Labor Force Statistics from the Current Population Survey. *Recuperado de: http://www. bls. gov/web/empsit/cpseea06. htm.*

Cizek, G. J., & Burg, S. S. (2006). *Addressing test anxiety in a high-stakes environment: Strategies for classrooms and schools.* Corwin Press.

Clinedinst, M. E., Hurley, S. F., & Hawkins, D. A. (2011). State of college admission. *Washington, DC: National Association for College Admission Counseling.*

De Fabrique, N. (2011). Section 504 of the Rehabilitation Act of 1973. In *Encyclopedia of Clinical Neuropsychology* (pp. 2227-2228). Springer New York.

Evans, J. (Ed.). (2017). *Equality, education, and physical education* (Vol. 21). Routledge.

Herrnstein, R. J., & Murray, C. (2010). *Bell curve: Intelligence and class structure in American life.* Simon and Schuster.

Kochhar-Bryant, C. A., & Izzo, M. V. (2006). Access to Post—High School Services: Transition Assessment and the Summary of Performance. *Career Development for Exceptional Individuals*, *29*(2), 70-89.

McCrea, B. (2014). Flipping the Classroom for Special Needs Students: Technology Can Play a Key Role in Helping Students with Physical and Learning Disabilities Stay Involved in Class and at Home. *THE Journal (Technological Horizons In Education)*, *41*(6), 24.

National Center for O*NET Development. Interest Profiler (IP). O*NET RESOURCE CENTER. *My Next Move.* **https://www.onetcenter.org/IP.html?p=2**

National Research Council. (2013). *Education for life and work: Developing transferable knowledge and skills in the 21st century.* National Academies Press.

Pauk, W., & Owens, R. J. (2013). *How to study in college.* Cengage Learning.

Rodriguez, P. D., & Marcum, G. D. (2016). Study habits, motives, and strategies of college students with symptoms of ADHD. *Journal of attention disorders*, *20*(9), 775-781.

Sheets, B.R. & Tilson, L.D. (2016) Learning transferable competencies/skills in the college classroom. Business Education Innovation Journal, 8(1), 67-71.

Venable, M. (2011). Adaptive Learning Technology: An Introduction. *Web-site: http://www. onlinecollege. org/20*, *11*, 08-30.

Week, E. (2011). Achievement gap. *Retrieved January*, *7*, 2012.

APPENDIX B

Websites

ACT   **www.act.org**

Bureau of Labor Statistics   **www.bls.gov**

Common Application   **www.commonapp.org**

Direct Student Loans   **www.studentsloans.gov**

Education Commission of the United States   **www.ecs.org**

FAFSA   **www.fafsa.ed.gov**

National Merit Program   **www.collegeboard.com**

O'NET Resource Center   **www.onetcenter.org**

Made in the USA
Columbia, SC
17 September 2020